Christmas Meditations

By Cologero Salvo

LIBER ESSE, SCIENTIAM ACQUIRERE, VERITATEM LOQUI

Copyright © 2017 Gornahoor Press All rights reserved

www.GornahoorPress.com

Logo and motto are service marks and trademarks of Gornahoor Press.

Revised 2018

TABLE OF CONTENTS

Advent Meditations 5
  Week One: Concentration without Effort 5
    Christian Yoga 5
    Concentration 7
    Contemplation 8
  Week Two: Purity of Thought 8
    Crown of Thorns 10
    Overcoming Negativity 12
  Week Three: Purity of Will 13
    Image and Likeness 14
    Emotions 15
    Purity of Heart is to Will One Thing 16
  Week Four: Incarnation of the Logos 17
    Spiritual Beings 19
Christmas Meditations 21
  The Infancy Narratives 21
    Salvation 22
    Death and Destiny 24
    Genealogy and World History 25
  The Herald Angels Sing 26
    The God of the Human Race 27
    Horizontal and Vertical Heredity 28
    Joseph's Role 28
    The Shepherds 30
  Revelation to the Wise 31
    Pagan Prophecies 31

- The Magi 32
- Wisdom 32
- The Star 34
- Appendix 36
  - Meditation on the Immaculate Conception 36
  - Incarnation of the Logos 38
  - Birth of the Logos in the Soul 39
  - Meditation on the Incarnation 40
    - The Path of Affirmation 41
    - The World Process 43
    - Creation and Redemption 44
  - Have You Ever Drunk the Silence? 45
  - Christmas and the Winter Solstice 47
  - Psychology of Mystical Experience 48
    - Animism 49
    - Metaphysical Awakening 50
    - Dualism and Pessimism 51
    - Pantheistic Monism 51
    - Monotheism and Supernatural Mysticism 53
    - Summary 54

ADVENT MEDITATIONS

Because the same One, who is begotten and born of God the Father, without ceasing in eternity, is born today, within time, in human nature, we make a holiday to celebrate it. St. Augustine says that this birth is always happening. And yet, if it does not occur in me, how could it help me? Everything depends on that. ~ **Meister Eckhart**

Thus, in the gospel He speaks through the flesh; and this sounded outwardly in the ears of men, **that it might be believed and sought inwardly**, and that *it might be found in the eternal Truth, where the good and only Master teaches all His disciples.* ~ **St Augustine**

Week One: Concentration without Effort

Christian Yoga

Valentin Tomberg, in *Letter II: The High Priestess* from *Meditations on the Tarot*, refers to the "second birth" as *Christian Yoga*. Hence, the elements of Christian Yoga are analogous to the stages of yoga described by **Patanjali** in the *Yoga Sutras*. In *Letter XVI: The Tower of Destruction*, these stages are related to the three stages of the spiritual life described by St. John of the Cross. Hence, we have this schema relating the yoga stages to the Christian stages:

Stages of Christian Yoga

Sanskrit	Greek	English	Spiritual Life
Dharana	Catharsis	Concentration	Purification
Dhyana	Theoria	Meditation	Illumination
Samadhi	Theosis	Contemplation	Mystical Union

Tomberg contrasts the Vedantic ideal with the Christian goal. The former, he says, leads to the extinction of consciousness, whereas the Christian goal is the "unity of two". For more on the differences between Yoga and Christianity, there is *Studies in the Psychology of the Mystics* by **Joseph Marechal, S.J** (see Appendix).

The Greek Mystic **Nicholas Cabasilas** in *The Life in Christ* explains that there are three obstacles to theosis. These are:

1. **Nature**. The Divine nature is different from human nature.
2. **Sin**. A will corrupted by evil separate us from God.
3. **Death**. In the mortal body, we can see only the dim reflection in the mirror; in this state our bodies are dominated by sense life.

These obstacles are overcome by the following historical events respectively:

1. **Incarnation**. This unites the human and divine natures in one person.
2. **Crucifixion**. The leads to the forgiveness of sins.
3. **Resurrection**. This overcomes death and the attraction to sense life.

Cabasilas relates these ideas to the effects of the sacraments, or mysteries, with the aim of salvation. The esoteric path aims beyond this to liberation. That aim is union while still in the mortal body:

1. Purify our soul so it becomes the perfect reflector of the Holy Spirit.
2. Expose our false sense of I, replaced with the mind of Christ.
3. Move from a life of instinct to a life of intelligence and love.

Concentration

We begin the process of purification by learning to concentrate, in particular, concentration without effort. A simple exercise is to focus attention on a part of the body, since it is the most stable part of our being. This may be deliberate or they may occur spontaneously throughout the day. During those moments of concentration, we can observe the automatic movements of thoughts, images, passions, personal desires, and other mental perturbations. The idea is to develop the ability to consciously direct attention, rather than to allow our attention to be randomly attracted.

We can observe, then, what happens to mental perturbations while we are directing attention. Is there Silence where there was previously "noise"? We can learn to maintain this concentration for longer periods, as Tomberg describes:

> To begin with there are moments, subsequently minutes, then "quarters of an hour" for which complete silence or "concentration without effort" lasts. With time, the silence or concentration without effort becomes a fundamental element *always present* in the life of the soul.

This concentration exercise is always available to us

whenever we remember to try it.

Contemplation

Mary of Agreda, in *The Mystical City of God*, reveals higher forms of concentration:

> Man's mind is rapt by God to the contemplation of the divine truth in three ways:
>
> 1. He contemplates it through certain imaginary pictures.
> 2. He contemplates the divine truth through its intelligible effects.
> 3. He contemplates it in its essence.
>
> Now when man's intellect is uplifted to the sublime vision of God's essence, it is necessary that his mind's whole attention should be summoned to that purpose in such a way that he understands nothing else by phantasms, and is absorbed entirely in God.

These ways are related to the stages of prayer: vocal prayer, mental prayer, and unceasing prayer.

- Concentration on mental images or thoughts are forms of meditation.
- Concentration that is beyond images and thoughts is contemplation.

Week Two: Purity of Thought

The distinguishing mark of the Hermetic path is that it seeks to make dogmas and teachings "real" in consciousness or the psyche. For some sceptics, this may sound as though it is "all in your mind," so that a psychological explanation explains the phenomena away. Carl Jung offers a deeper explanation:

> What most people overlook or seem unable to understand is the fact that I regard the psyche as *real*. ... Religious statements have to do with the reality of the *psyche*.

In this spirit, we can meditate more fully on the meaning of **Christmas**.

- The birth in the past of Christ the Redeemer.
- The expectation of Christ the Judge at the end of time.
- The birth of Christ in the soul eternally, now.

Redemption is the reversal of the effects of the Fall. The Hermetic Tradition calls this process "regeneration" as we seek to make that real in consciousness. The undoing of the Fall requires the second birth of Christ/Logos in the soul. That is, the soul, as the passive element, reflects the activity of the Spirit. Disturbances in the soul — resulting from passions, images, desires, thoughts — will distort the image of the Spirit, just as disturbances on a pond distort its reflection of the surrounding forest.

It is the personal, subjective element that is at the root of such disturbances. Thus, the solution is to become more objective about oneself. That requires taking the standpoint of Christ the Judge. Justice is possible only when the Judge is totally objective, not influenced by ignorance, opinion, personal preferences, vested interests, or subjective passions. **Valentin Tomberg** writes in this regard:

> The vow of *obedience* is the practice of silencing personal desires, emotions, and imagination in the face of reason and conscience; it is the primacy of the ideal as opposed to the apparent, the nation as opposed to the personal, humanity as opposed to the nation, and God as opposed to humanity. It is the life

of cosmic and human hierarchical ordering; it is the meaning and justification of the fact that there are Seraphim, Cherubim, Thrones; Dominions, Virtues, Powers; Principalities, Archangels, Angels; Priests, Knights and Commoners. Obedience is order: it is international law; it is the state; it is the Church; it is universal peace. True obedience is the very opposite of tyranny and slavery, since its root is the love which issues from faith and confidence. That which is above serves that which is below and that which is below obeys that which is above. Obedience is the practical conclusion to that which one recognises as the existence of something higher than oneself. Whosoever recognises God, obeys.

Yet that does not address the question of "how" to obey. We cannot obey as long as subjective elements have their grip on us; these are impure elements that disturb the soul. Tomberg discusses the idea of purity in the context of the five wounds and three vows. We can summarize these in two stages— purity of thought and purity of will. These correspond to the head and the heart respectively.

Crown of Thorns

Purity of thought is the "crown of thorns". The following passages explain that symbol:

> Thus every crown is essentially a crown of thorns. Not only is it heavy, but also it calls for a painful restraint with regard to the thought and free or arbitrary imagination of the personality.
>
> Here true thought receives confirmation and subsequent illumination; false or irrelevant thought is riveted and reduced to impotence. The crown of the Emperor signifies the renunciation of freedom of intellectual movement, just as his arms and legs

signify his renunciation of freedom of action and movement. He is deprived of the three so-called "natural" liberties of the human being — those of opinion, word, and movement.

The "crown of thorns" is borne, in principle, by every person capable of *objective* thought — the "crown of thorns" being given to the human being since the beginning of human history.

The lack of concentration allows arbitrary, free, and irrelevant thoughts and images to flourish in our consciousness. We need to renounce them so they can be replaced by true thoughts; the art of concentration will help in that regard.

Nicholas Cabasilas writes this in his commentary on the beatitude of "purity of heart".

> To cleanse one's heart and to exercise one's soul for sanctification—what striving or effort or exertion would effect this more than these thoughts and meditations? Yet, if one examines this carefully, one would not call it the effect of meditation on Christ, but rather of the meditation itself.
>
> To be occupied with the noblest of thoughts means to abandon evil thoughts; but this is to be pure in heart. Our life and our birth are twofold, both spiritual and fleshly. By its desires, the spirit fights against the body and the body resists the spirit. Since it is impossible for contraries to be at peace and to join together, it is quite evident that one or other of the desires will by means of memory, gain control over the thoughts and cast the other out. The memory of the life and birth which are according to the flesh and concentration on such matters produce the most depraved desires and the uncleanness to which it leads. So likewise, when the soul by constant remembrance holds fast the birth of the baptismal washing, the divine Food which is

appropriate to this birth, and the other things which belong to the new life, it is likely to lead desires from the earth to heaven itself.

We can extract these main points:

- There is our fleshly birth in the body and a second spiritual birth.
- There is an inner spiritual battle between lower (personal, subjective) thoughts and higher (spiritual, objective) thoughts.
- "Constant remembrance" is necessary. In our terms, this is constant awareness, "concentration without effort".

Hermetically, this movement from fleshly to spiritual thoughts is a mystical evolution. This is the regeneration of the inner life from the Instincts to fully human life of the Intellect and Intuition.

Overcoming Negativity

The task for this week is to work on the purity of thought.

Whenever we catch ourselves harbouring negative or hateful thoughts about others, envious thoughts, inappropriate erotic thoughts, *inter alia*, even negative thoughts—perhaps especially—about ourselves, we are to do the concentration exercise.

Bring attention to your selected body area and while you maintain that awareness, observe those thoughts while striving—without effort—and see what happens.

We need to be gatekeeper's of our thoughts, like an esoteric version of Maxwell's Demon.

There is a small tension in the birth of Christ in the soul. On the one hand, we are to judge our thoughts objectively and impartially, like Christ the Judge. We shouldn't want to be burdened by negativity.

On the other hand, Christ the Redeemer, will forgive (under the appropriate circumstances) these negative thoughts. There is the tendency in the modern world, under the influence of Freud and the "masters of suspicion" to consider negativity as representing "what we really are" or "our *true* feelings". Quite the contrary ... they are usually temptations from lower forces, not what we are meant to be.

Week Three: Purity of Will

It is futile to attempt to be concentrated if the Will is passionate about other things. The oscillations of the mind will never be able to achieve silence unless the Will itself infuses it with silence. Only the still Will can render the imagination and the intellect silent in concentration.

> **St. John of the Cross** and **St. Theresa d'Avila** never tire of repeating that the concentration necessary for spiritual prayer is the fruit of the **moral purification of the Will**. ~ **Valentin Tomberg**, *Meditations on the Tarot*

Concentration can be applied on three planes:

- Mental
- Astral
- Physical

We began with learning concentration on the physical plane. Then we transferred that knowledge to our thoughts or mental plane. Finally, we will do the same to our emotional life for the purification of the soul.

Note that there are many more levels beyond these. In the *Letter XVII: The Star*, Tomberg explains:

> There are *twelve* degrees higher than that of the consciousness of the human transcendental Self. It is necessary, therefore, in order to attain to the ONE God, to elevate oneself successively to degrees of consciousness of the nine spiritual hierarchies and the Holy Trinity.

The Mental, Astral, and Physical correspond to the spirit, soul, and body. In *Letter XX: The Judgment*, Tomberg relates them to the Trinity. The undivided self, then, corresponds to the Unity of God.

Image and Likeness

The idea of man being the "image and likeness" of God is a recurrent theme throughout *Meditations on the Tarot*. Although people today often like to repeat that we are all born in the "image and likeness" of God, that is not at all the Traditional teaching. We retain the image of God but, because of the Fall, we have lost the full likeness and it is the task of the Hermetist to restore it. Tomberg explains:

> The ideal of alchemical *transformation* of Hermetism offers to human beings the way to the realisation of true human nature, which is the image and likeness of God. Hermetism is the re-humanisation of all elements of human nature; it is their return to their true essence. Just as all base metals can be transformed into silver and into gold, so are all the forces of human nature susceptible to transformation into "silver" or "gold", i.e. into what they *are* when they share in the image and likeness of God.

If we are already in the "image and likeness of God", then our level of being as such right now is perfect: i.e., there is no need for transformation, redemption, or regeneration.

The image of God, according to **St. Bernard**, is our

"essential" being. In that case it must be our intellectual soul, which distinguishes humans from animals. It is unsullied, it has no negative part, it is free, it is the source of the "spark of God", and so is perfect. However, we rarely live at that level of awareness. It is as though we own a penthouse suite, yet choose to live in the basement.

The likeness, on the other hand, is our soul life which reflects the image. This is—because of the various perturbations—what must be purified.

Emotions

As was mentioned last time, personal emotions need to be silenced to make the soul capable of "receiving from above the revelation of the word, the life and the light."

Now, the emotional centre of our being, or the "astral" plane, has its own way of knowing. This is called the "cognitive power of the emotions". This manner of knowing is quite different from that of the thinking centre or mental plane. This knowing is *episteme*, the knowledge of the heart, beyond the *dianoia* of mental knowing. There is a higher emotional component concomitant with its knowing.

Our age is dominated by thinking, arguing, and so on. This dualistic thinking distorts the emotional centre. Tomberg writes this about the relationship between the will and thinking:

> Thus, it is not thought as such which allows the desire for personal greatness or the tendency towards megalomania, but rather *the will* which makes use of the head and which can take hold of thought and reduce it to the role of its instrument.
>
> *Organic* humility, replacing the current of the will-to-greatness is not found in the head, but rather in the heart, i.e. it reaches the heart, penetrating from the

right-hand side. Because it is there that the will-to-greatness has its origin and it is there from whence it takes hold of the head and makes it its instrument. This is why many thinkers and scientists want to think "without the heart" in order to be objective, which is an illusion, because one can in no way think without the heart, the heart being the activating principle of thought; what one can do is to think with a humble and warm heart instead of with a pretentious and cold heart.

When functioning well, the heart and the head cooperate. In the example of megalomania, on the other hand, we see that the will can take hold of the head, making it the servant of a disordered emotion. Common sense warns us about making decisions when in a negative emotional state, but that is often ignored. Moreover, it is even celebrated, since an opinion stated with strong negative emotions is falsely given a higher value.

The other distortion is when the head tries to think without the heart under the guise of objectivity. This leaves our emotional range limited and underdeveloped.

Purity of Heart is to Will One Thing

The inner life of the soul, in our present condition, does not present a unity. Rather, our desires, aspirations, passions, and so on, are in conflict with each other. First one dominates, then another, as though there were multiple separate "I's" inhabiting, and even fighting for control over, the soul. Tomberg calls these "lost sheep" alluding to the Gospel story. He explains:

> The soul's faults and vices are not, fundamentally, monsters but rather, lost sheep. ... As it is the same with all the soul's faults and vices, we all have the mission of finding and bringing back to the flock (i.e.

to the soul's choral harmony) the lost sheep in ourselves. We are missionaries in the subjective domain of our own soul, charged with the task of the conversion of our desires, ambitions, etc. We have to *persuade* them that they are seeking the realisation of their dreams in a false way by showing them the true way. It is not a matter of commandment, but rather of the alchemy of the cross, i.e. making present an alternative way for our desires, ambitions, passions, etc. It is a matter, moreover, of the alchemical "marriage of opposites".

Our alchemical task, then, is the transmutation of these multiple selves into a single I, the process of Individuation.

Week Four: Incarnation of the Logos

The tendency is certainly accentuated, if not prevalent, amongst contemporary Hermetists to occupy themselves more with the "Cosmic Christ" or the "Logos" than with the human person of the "Son of Man", Jesus of Nazareth. More importance is attributed to the divine and abstract aspect of the God-Man than to his human and concrete aspect.

It was contact with the person of Jesus Christ which opened up the current of miracles and conversions. And it is the same even today. ~ **Valentin Tomberg**, *Letter VIII: Justice*

With these words, Tomberg is warning us not to forget about the first coming of Jesus in the flesh, regarded as somehow inferior to an esoteric interpretation. A fortiori, the Hermetist's goal is not to create an alternative or "better" religion. Nevertheless, there is always a stream of "New Age" gurus who claim something similar. For example, one such popular guru claims to have discovered the real meaning of all the religions, viz., what the Buddha "really" taught or what

Christ "really" taught. He then claims that the religions have distorted those teachings and offer no authentic path. Although he came to that realization spontaneously, he will teach you certain "modalities" for a hefty price to reach the same realization. This is the sin of simony, the notion that spiritual enlightenment is a commodity that can be bought and sold.

The idea of the Logos was not unknown to pagan philosophers and Hermetists prior to the first Christmas. However, it is the fact of the Incarnation that matters most, as St John pointed out in the remarkable claim that the Logos became flesh. So Jesus is not only the fulfilment of the Mosaic law, He is also the fulfilment of the natural law. This is made clear by the visit of the Magi.

Tomberg makes us wrestle with a philosophical conundrum. The thinking mind, restricted to dianoia, knows essences, and the Logos is "the fundamental universal [or essence] of the world". And Jesus Christ is then the "particular of particulars". Some minds, like that of the new age guru, see that as representing a limitation on their thought; hence they resort to a sort of Docetism which denies the need for the physical, including a birth, a visible church, sacraments, and so on. It is a small step, then, to reach the conclusion that there is no need for the purification of the head and the heart in order to reach higher states.

Since for God, essence and existence are One, to know God is to know both his essence and existence. Tomberg explains that

> Christian Hermetism itself can only be knowledge of the universal which is revealed in the particular.

Hence, the Christian Hermetist "aspires to mystical experience of the communion of beings through love". Thus he seeks spiritual friendships in the particular.

Yet, not unlike the pagan Hermetists—his precursors—or

even the New Ager perhaps, he also seeks the mystical experience of communion with the Logos, i.e., the knowledge of the universal.

Spiritual Beings

Fr. Reginald Garrigou-Lagrange tells us that the angels know intuitively, not rationally. Each higher level of angel understands more through the knowledge of ever more encompassing principles. Tomberg asserts:

> For Hermetism there are no "principles", "laws" and "ideas" which exist outside of individual beings, not as structural traits of their nature, but as entities separated and independent from it.

This makes perfect sense, since knowing and being are one. If an angel, then, "knows" a certain principle, he is *ipso facto* the embodiment of that principle. Ideas have no power of their own, they are purely passive. An idea has effects only when it is immanent in a being. We can choose to understand our environment as an abstraction, the mere interplay of impersonal forces. Or else, we can choose to understand it as a great drama of personal forces.

A recent episode of the Vikings series on the History Channel had an interesting scene. Rollo was a Viking warrior who converted to Catholicism and was rewarded with the Duchy of Normandy. Unable to totally forget his pagan past, he explained to his wife, "When you hear thunder, it is only thunder. But when I hear thunder, I hear the sound of Thor." This is reminiscent of what Owen Barfield called Original Participation.

Tomberg tells us we must "love our pagan past", so perhaps we can learn something from Rollo. Now this is not a new teaching, but actually something we forgot. So perhaps we can try to remember. The mystic visionary, Catherine Emmerich, saw that the world was populated with angels: each country, city, diocese, and parish has its own guardian angel. Furthermore, each generation has "generational spirits", not all benign, as a sort of Zeitgeist, or "spirit of the age".

If we can overcome the Zeitgeist of scientism, we can meditate on our role in the cosmic hierarchy. See yourself in relation to your family, parish or other community, nation, Church, then ascending through the angelic hierarchy. And when you get to the Logos, see also the Baby in the manger.

CHRISTMAS MEDITATIONS

The Infancy Narratives

This is a review of *The Infancy Narratives* by **Joseph Ratzinger**. Since the story is, or should be, very familiar, we want to instead focus more on the exegetical methods used by Fr. Ratzinger than on the story itself. He writes that good exegesis involves two stages.

1. **Historical component**. What did the authors intend to convey through their text in their own day?
2. **Contemporary component**. Is it true? Does it concern me? How so?

Obviously, spiritual writings do not concern me in the same way as a new tax code might. Unlike a subject like chemistry, for example, spiritual truths are best communicated through myths and symbols. As such, their meaning—their "concern for me"—are not always open to everyone. That is because they describe "spiritual processes that have given birth to a new people" [J J Bachofen].

That is true in regard to the narratives surrounding the birth of Jesus. Nevertheless, these narratives also claim to be representing "the history of events occurring materially on earth". There are two easy, but ultimately unhelpful, solutions (beyond complete rejection):

- Accept the spiritual teaching but not the material. Christ, then, is one of the world's great teachers. This superficially sounds more "intellectual", since it avoids the messiness of actual events.
- Naively accept the historical aspect without a deeper concern. This is the sentimental solution. Unfortunately, facts are mute and do

not speak for themselves. Hence, there is the need for a careful exegesis of the type taught us by Fr. Ratzinger.

We have the model of **Marius Victorinus**, the Neoplatonic philosopher who initially accepted Christianity as an intellectual system, but not as a historical teaching with institutions, and so on. Or perhaps the Inklings, like C. S. Lewis and Tolkein, had a better idea: it is a myth that actually happened. Here, we will take the perspective of Victorinus. The historical component will have to be an individual decision.

In the first part, we highlight Fr. Ratzinger's exegetical points, drawing out their logical consequences, and placing them into a larger perspective. The second part will focus on the birth of Jesus and the revelation to the shepherds. The final part concerns the Magi on the feast of the Epiphany.

Salvation

Perhaps we no longer consciously think in terms of a saviour, but at the time of Jesus' birth, the idea of a saviour was in the air. This, for example, was written about Augustus Caesar, the Emperor at the time:

> Providence, which has ordered all things, filled [Augustus] with virtue that he might benefit mankind, sending him as a Saviour ... the birthday of the god was the beginning of the good tidings that he brought for the world. From his birth, a new reckoning of time must begin.

Fr. Ratzinger points out that religion and politics were not separated as they are now. Salvation then also included peace, a recurring theme in the Christmas message. Yet, a political solution is not the point. In *Introduction to Christianity*, Fr. Ratzinger describes the situation of man, which has been called "original sin".

> The seat of original sin is to be sought precisely in this collective net that precedes the individual existence as a sort of spiritual datum, not in any biological legacy passed on between otherwise utterly separated individuals. ... no man can start from scratch any more, completely unimpaired by history. No one starts off in an unimpaired condition in which he would only need to develop himself freely and lay out his own grounds; everyone lives in a web that is a part of his existence itself.

In other words, we inherit this structure. This is not biological heredity, otherwise it would be a medical problem. That is, a "physician of the body" could develop a serum, a vaccine, a surgical procedure, or a genetic recoding to "cure" original sin. So original sin must be a defect of the soul, not directly the body. **Rene Guenon** states how this is possible, while still being inheritable:

> That there is a psychic heredity as well as a physiological heredity is hardly in doubt and is even a fact of common observation. But what few take into account is that at the least it supposes that the parents furnish a psychic seed as well as a biological seed. (*The Psychic Fallacy*, p 176)

So salvation can come only from a *physician of the soul*, a designation for Christ. The world system cannot be cured from within. With the knowledge of good and evil, man learned to separate the "no" from the "yes", the false from the true, evil from good, doubt instead of faith. The influences of the world are legion and contradict each other. Only a transcendent influence from above can be the source of salvation. So being enters history. **Boris Mouravieff** identifies the world system as the "A" influences and the transcendent as the "B" influences.

Death and Destiny

In his analysis of the symbolism of Ocnus the Rope Plaiter found in a tomb, **J J Bachofen** describes the pagan worldview revealed therein, in these terms:

> The thread of death is woven into the web of which every tellurian organism consists. Death is the supreme natural law, the *fatum* of material life, to which the gods themselves bow, which they cannot claim to master. Thus the web of tellurian creation becomes the web of destiny, the thread becomes the carrier of human fate ... the loom, carrier of the supreme law of creation written in the stars, was assigned to the Uranian deities in their sidereal nature; and, finally, that human life and the entire cosmos were seen as a great web of destiny.

The radicalness of the new message cannot be known unless and until one can place oneself in the place of the pagans at that time, fully feeling or recreating in his interiority the weight of this heavy conception of death and destiny. The pagan view, as exemplified, for example, in Plato and Hinduism, was entirely moralistic. A person was rewarded or punished after his death in accordance with his acts while alive. This judgment was impersonal and mechanical, the *lex talionis*, "an eye for an eye". In contrast, the new message is one of life and freedom, not death and destiny. Fr Ratzinger recounts **Bernard of Clarivaux**'s sermon on the topic:

> After the error of our first parents, the whole world was shrouded in darkness, under the dominion of death. Now God seeks to enter the world anew. He knocks at Mary's door. He needs human freedom. The only way he can redeem man, who was created free, is by means of a free "yes" to his will. In creating freedom, he made himself in a certain sense dependent upon man. His power is tied to the unenforceable "yes" of a human being".

Thus God is revealed both as Being and as acting in history, transcendent and immanent. Unlike the pagan gods who themselves were subject to death and destiny, God is revealed as the creator of the cosmos. No longer subject to the stars, man becomes free. So free, in fact, that the salvation of the world depends first on Mary's free choice. Only in freedom can there be an escape from the domination of worldly influences. In *Introduction to Christianity*, Fr. Ratzinger writes:

> Only by the action of the individual can the transformation of history, the destruction of the *dictatorship or the milieu* come to pass.

This "dictatorship of the milieu" is the set of worldly influences.

Genealogy and World History

Even to the casual reader, Matthew's and Luke's genealogies differ from each other in significant ways. Rather than engage in hypothetical contortions to harmonize them, Fr. Ratzinger makes another choice. Anyone familiar with esoteric texts will recognize that deliberate contradictions indicate that the text is to be understood symbolically, not literally. Hence, Fr. Ratzinger brings out the symbolic meaning of the two accounts.

Matthew starts with Abraham and leads forward to Jesus, in three sets of 14 generations each. Curiously, he points out that the number for the name "David" is 14, giving force to the idea that Jesus is the heir of David. This is the only place where Kabbalistic numerology is used, but this can be understood as a tacit endorsement of that method.

So for Matthew, Abraham is the beginning of the history with Jesus as the fulfilment. The first phase of 14 generations leads from Abraham to David; the second phase, a period of decline leading to the Babylonian captivity; and the third, rises again to Jesus. However, Joseph, while the legal father, is not mentioned as the "begetter" of Jesus, who was instead born of Mary. So legally he belongs to the house of David, but his origin is elsewhere, begotten from above. The idea of vertical and horizontal heredity will be discussed again in the third segment

Luke, on the other hand, starts with Jesus as an adult and then works the genealogy backward to Adam. This indicates the Jesus is a new orientation to world history. Adam transcended animality by being made in the image and likeness of God. Jesus, on the other hand, is the god-man. The god-man transcends man just as fully as Adam transcended the animal. We, then, are offered the opportunity to achieve *theosis*, to truly become god-like. Thus the unfulfilled goal of both Adam and Plato, to be like the gods, finally becomes possible in world history.

The Herald Angels Sing

Relying on the best of recent biblical exegesis, Fr. **Joseph Ratzinger** provides interesting details regarding the actual birth of Jesus in Bethlehem. He avoids the sentimentalism often surrounding the Christmas story, and instead brings out its essential meaning. What I prefer to focus on here is the meaning rather than the events, which are familiar to all. In particular, God's revelation via angels brings out important details that are still helpful today. The method of this revelation was different for Mary, Joseph, and the Shepherds. These took the forms of command, dream, and song, respectively, all forms of communication that bypass the lower intellectual mind and pass directly to higher centres.

We have already discussed the annunciation to Mary. This came in the form of a command, not a logical proof nor a discussion. Such an incredible message could only take hold in a sinless consciousness, aligned already with the will of

God, and not beclouded by the "personal equation". There can be no debate; only the free choice between obedience and rebellion.

The God of the Human Race

In the myths of the origins of Rome, the idea of the birth of a god-man from the mating of a god with a virgin was not unknown in ancient time. Even the ancient Greek cities had their spiritual origin from a man they revered as a god. The god, in all those cases however, was the god of a specific people and bestowed a particular identifying spiritual gift on them. However, as Fr. Ratzinger points out, such myths created a mixed being, a demi-god, whereas Christ was fully God and fully man, without confusion or mixture. Moreover, unlike the timeless quality of a myth, this story is determined at a specific place and time.

So the meaning of the birth of Jesus is different. The Holy Spirit, from whom Jesus was conceived, is the "giver of life" itself, not just one aspect of life. He is the God of the human race, not just of a particular people. Nevertheless, such a possibility was known to a few people at that time:

> As to the god of the human race, a few philosophers had an idea of him; the mysteries of Eleusis might have afforded a glimpse of him to the most intelligent of the initiated; but the vulgar never believed in such a god. ~ **Fustel de Coulanges**, *The Ancient City*

With the birth of Jesus, this God was revealed to all. The revelation to the vulgar will be described in this chapter in regard to the shepherds. The revelation to the initiated will be the topic of the following chapter on the Magi.

Horizontal and Vertical Heredity

While Luke traces the genealogy of Jesus horizontally back to Adam, the first man, John indicates the vertical origin of Jesus as the incarnation of the Logos. Analogously, the birth of each human being is the result of both horizontal and vertical heredity. In horizontal heredity, the physical and psychic characteristics of the ancestors are transmitted to the descendants. In the vertical dimension, the intellectual soul, or individuality, is breathed into the body/soul.

This is explained more fully by **Valentin Tomberg** in Letter XX of *Meditations on the Tarot*. Horizontal heredity operates by imitation of the ancestors. As Fr. Ratzinger points out, we are born into a "collective net" of our ancestors, tracing back to the very origins of the human race. The unravelling of this net requires the birth of the perfect man. Only then can we experience a second birth, as adopted children of God, which lifts us out of and liberates us from that net. We see this in John:

> To all who received him, who believed in his name, he gave power to become children of God, who were born, not of blood, nor of the will of the flesh, nor of the will of man, but of God. ~ John 1:12-13

Joseph's Role

Since Joseph's role is often given short shrift, it is useful to focus on what Fr. Ratzinger writes about him:

> Whereas the angel "came" to Mary, he merely appears to Joseph in a dream ... Once again this shows us an essential quality of the figure of Saint Joseph:
>
> - his capacity to perceive the divine and
> - his ability to discern.

> Only a man who is inwardly watchful for the divine, only someone with a real sensitivity for God and his ways, can receive God's message in this way.

Obviously, what was revealed in Joseph's dream was quite difficult to believe. So how was Joseph able to discern God's will, even as revealed in a dream? That is because Joseph was a just, or righteous, man, and a just man is one whose life is lived in and from the word of God. Also, Joseph was "inwardly watchful", that is, he monitored and guarded his thoughts. He was able to see past the trap of the collective net of human influences to recognize the divine influences that transcended them.

Of course, many people ask God for a "sign" to reveal His will for them. But are they just? Could they really recognize God's message, given their spiritual state? Or do they prejudge the sign so that only something consoling or beneficial is interpreted as a sign? Fr. Ratzinger offers this challenge:

> God is constantly regarded as a limitation placed on our freedom that must be set aside if man is ever to be completely himself. God, with his truth, stands in opposition to man's manifold lies, his self-seeking and his pride. God is love. But love can also be hated when it challenges us to transcend ourselves. It is not a romantic "good feeling". Redemption is not "wellness", it is not about basking in self-indulgence; on the contrary, it is liberation from the imprisonment in self-absorption.

A duty of the father is to name the son. This name, "Jesus", was revealed to Joseph. It means "Yahweh is salvation". The angel in the dream explains: "He will save his people from their sins." Since this is the purpose of the incarnation, it is imperative to understand exactly what that means. Fr. Ratzinger explains:

> Man is a relational being. And if his first, fundamental relationship is disturbed—his relationship with

> God—than nothing else can be truly in order. This is where the priority lies in Jesus' message and ministry: before all else, he wants to point man toward the essence of his malady ... if you are not healed there, then however many good things you may find, you are not truly healed.

Clearly, it is not simply a matter of "doing good", as Plato thought, or of avoiding certain behaviours. Rather, sin is the state of not being in proper relationship with God, the Logos.

The Shepherds

Shepherds were in the fields around the region where Jesus was born, "keeping watch over their flocks by night." Once again, we see the theme of watchfulness. The shepherds were not just outwardly close to the event, but "they were also inwardly closer to the event, unlike the peacefully sleeping townsfolk. ... inwardly they were not far from the God who had become a child." The watchfulness of the shepherds has become part of the monastic tradition.

When the angel appears to the shepherds, they were filled with fear. Just as the angel Gabriel reassured Mary not to fear, the angel likewise dispels the shepherds' fear. The spirit of fear is the opposite of the spirit of love.

Then a multitude of angels appeared praising God: "Glory to God in the highest, and on earth peace among men with whom he is pleased." Fr. Ratzinger makes this fascinating point:

> Christianity has always understood that the speech of angels is actually song, in which all the glory of the great joy that they proclaim becomes tangibly present.

As **Julian Jaynes** documented in *The Origin of Consciousness in the Breakdown of the Bicameral Mind*, speech in the forms of commands, music, and poetry bypasses the rational mind. Specifically, there is a direct revelation or intuition, without the duality of yes/no, faith/doubt, etc. Even among the Greeks, the muses sang the poetry, so that they were literally heard.

So the true experience of angels is not dualistic, and not even visual. The angelic song goes straight to the shepherds' hearts, not their heads.

Revelation to the Wise

> Revelation presupposes emptiness—space put at its disposal—in order to manifest itself. This is why it is necessary to renounce. ~ **Valentin Tomberg**

> The concept of first-born takes on a cosmic dimension. Christ, the incarnate Son, is God's first thought, preceding all creation, which is ordered toward him and proceeds from him. He is both the beginning and the goal of the new creation. ~ **Joseph Ratzinger**

Pagan Prophecies

Balaam was a pagan soothsayer, quoted in the Bible. He would have used auguries to arrive at his prophecies. This is what he prophesied about Israel:

> I see him, but not now; I behold him, but not nigh: a star shall come forth out of Jacob and a sceptre shall rise out of Israel (Numbers 24:17)

This prophecy about a star and a king was known to other nations outside Israel. Some of them may have pondered about the new "king of the Jews" and how to recognize him. The point here is that boundaries were not as strict as we may assume today. A pagan, since he was quoted in the Bible, could experience a divine revelation. Although Fr. Ratzinger does not mention it, there are parallels between Zoroaster and Moses.

The Magi

The Magi were from the "land of sunrise", i.e., the East. They were members of the Persian priestly caste, presumably the Zoroastrian religion. The Magi were also the teachers of the Greek philosophers. Aristotle mentioned the Magi, and he also believed that the Hebrews originated in India where they were called "Kalani".

On the one hand, the Magi were seekers of truth. On the other, they could also be the possessors of supernatural knowledge who used their powers to deceive and seduce (See Acts 13:10.) This reflects the difference between sacred magic and personal magic. (See *Letter V: The Pope*.) The Magi of Matthew's Gospel are of the former type and use "religious and philosophical wisdom as an incentive to set off in the right direction, it is the wisdom that ultimately leads people to Christ."

Wisdom

Besides Baalam's prophecy, according to Tacitus and Suetonius, there was speculation at that time that the ruler of the world would emerge from Judah. Fr. Ratzinger speculates about the Magi:

> They were people of inner unrest, people of hope, people on the lookout for the true star of salvation. The men of whom Matthew speaks were not just astronomers. They were "wise". They represent the inner dynamic of religion toward self-transcendence, which involves a search for truth, a search for the true God and hence "philosophy" in the original sense of the word. Wisdom, then, serves to purify the message

of science: the rationality of that message does not remain at the level of intellectual knowledge, but seeks understanding in its fullness and so raises reason to its loftiest possibilities.

We have seen revelation in various guises. There was the revelation to Mary who was sinless, to Joseph who was just, and to the Shepherds, who were spiritually poor and watchful. Finally, we have the revelation to the intelligent, beautifully expressed. Fr. Ratzinger shows us the proper use of intelligence. This is how he described the qualities of God:

> We may not ascribe to God anything nonsensical or irrational, or anything that contradicts His creation.

So to become more God-like, we need to strive to be sensible, rational, and consistent. *Pace* certain irrationalists and fideists, the true religion is not irrational, although it transcends reason. Rene Guenon asserts nothing different.

Fr. Ratzinger makes some important affirmations. The Magi represent certain types, from which he concludes:

- They represent the religions moving toward Christ.
- They represent the self-transcendence of science toward him.
- They are the successors of Abraham who set off on a journey in response to God's call.
- They are the successors of Socrates and his habit of questioning above and beyond conventional religion toward the higher truth.

In summary, Christ is not just the fulfilment of the religion of the Hebrews, but also that of the pagans. He is known not just to the priests and prophets, but also to the philosophers and scientists.

> The key point is this: the wise men from the east are a new beginning. They represent the journeying of humanity toward Christ. They initiate a procession

that continues throughout history. Not only do they represent the people who have found the way to Christ: they represent the inner aspiration of the human spirit, the dynamism of religions and human reason toward him.

The Star

It is seldom helpful to speculate about likely, or more often not-very-likely, stories to try to harmonize theological accounts with alleged historical and scientific events. So rather than postulating some sort of supernova, there is another way to look at it. In any event, the reliance on a supernatural star destroys the whole inner meaning of the story, which depends on the inner attitude of the Magi, not some external compulsion.

In the year 7 BC (the most probable year for Jesus' birth), there was a conjunction of Jupiter and Saturn in the constellation Pisces (the Fish). Jupiter was the highest deity and would have been brightest in the evening alongside Saturn. Saturn represented the Jewish people, since Saturn was identified with Yahweh (they shared the same day of the week: Saturday). The Babylonian astronomers could conclude this: the birth in the land of the Jews of a ruler who would bring salvation. Of course, this was not compelling in itself, but depended on the Magi's inner state of expectation. Fr. Ratzinger writes:

> This implies that the cosmos speaks of Christ. The language of creation provides a great many pointers. It gives man an intuition of the Creator.

Here we can recall Guenon who wrote that Creation is the reflection of the Logos, the first Thought of God. This is the message to the wise. For others:

> The knowledge that emerges from creation, and acquires concrete form in the religions, can also become disoriented, so that it no longer prompts man to transcend himself, but induces him to lock himself into systems with which he believes he can, in some way, oppose the hidden powers of the world.

A further point is that astrology, at least as understood, came to an end with the Magi. The ancients regarded the heavenly bodies as divine powers determining men's fate. Now we understand that Christ conquered all the powers and forces in the heavens and reigns over the entire universe. It is not the star that determines the child's destiny, it is the child that directs the star.

Appendix

Meditation on the Immaculate Conception

One can also say that the incarnated human being is the product of two heredities—horizontal heredity and vertical heredity, the latter being the imprint of the individuality form above and the former being the imprint of the ancestors here below. This seeks to express that he is the product of two imitations—horizontal and vertical, i.e., that in order to become what he is, he owes it to imitation of his ancestors from the past and to that of himself above. In the last analysis, therefore, it is a matter on the one hand of horizontal heredity going back to the archetype or terrestrial heredity, i.e. Adam, and on the other hand of vertical heredity rising up to the Father who is heaven, i.e. God. This is why it is so important to allow light from the dogma of the **immaculate conception** to convince us of its truth, for what is at stake is the line of vertical heredity—"God-man heredity". ~ Valentin Tomberg

The Father gave her his Son, the Son came down into her virginal womb to become her child; in her the Holy Spirit miraculously fashioned the body of Jesus and made her soul his own dwelling place, penetrating her whole being in such an ineffable manner that the expression "Spouse of the Holy Spirit" is far from adequate to express the life of the Spirit in her and through her. In Jesus there are two natures, divine and human, but one single Person who is God; here on the contrary we have two natures and two persons, the Holy Spirit and the Immaculata, but united in a union that defies all human expression. ~ St. Maximilian Kolbe

> For the Word generated by the Father is understood by the one in whom it is received perfectly — by that person who is the Immaculate Conception. ~ St. Maximilian Kolbe
>
> By the power of the Holy Spirit the Word became incarnate from the Virgin Mary. ~ Nicene Creed

Just as Eve was the genetic equivalent to Adam, apart from the X chromosome, so likewise is the New Adam the genetic equivalent to the New Eve. In our time, given our knowledge of biology and genetics, the possibility of a virginal conception is no longer inconceivable.

So Jesus, the New Adam, is the genetic image of his Mother, Mary, the New Eve. Moreover, while the body of Jesus was in Mary's womb, her soul was, in Kolbe's words, the dwelling place of the Holy Spirit. As we saw in *Letter II: The High Priestess*, the Holy Spirit can be reflected only in the completely unperturbed soul, a soul protected from sin. That is Mary, who—free from sin—understood the Spirit perfectly.

As Tomberg points out, we are under the law of horizontal heredity, in imitation of our ancestors, going back to Adam. This prepares the biological and social environment into which the individuality can incarnate. Hence, Jesus appears at a specific time and place, to the mother prepared to receive him. She was free from original sin, and thereby was in the same state as Eve before the Fall.

While Mary was "full of grace" from the beginning, we are likewise called to be full of grace; this is *theosis*. This confirmed in Mary as the Queen of Heaven. For us, it is something to be achieved. For that, she is our model.

Jesus has two natures, divine and human, in one Person. We, through *theosis*, can have a divine as well as a human nature. However, we retain our own Person, so this union of the human with the divine requires two persons. By purifying our own soul, the Holy Spirit can become better and better reflected in our own consciousness. Then the Logos is born in us, too, and we put on our true Self:

> And I live, now not I; but Christ liveth in me. And that I live now in the flesh: I live in the faith of the Son of God, who loved me, and delivered himself for me. ~ Galations 2:20

Incarnation of the Logos

> In the beginning was the Word, and the Word was with God, and the Word was God. The same was in the beginning with God. All things were made by him: and without him was made nothing that was made. In him was life, and the life was the light of men. And the light shineth in darkness, and the darkness did not comprehend it. ~ **Gospel of John**

In this gospel passage, the birth of Christ is expressed in theological language, since the mere historical fact has no meaning in itself. For example, Meister Eckhart said that it was of little import to him if Jesus was born of Mary in history, if He is not born in him, here and now. In his words:

> What would it avail me if I had a brother who was a rich man, and for my part I were a poor man? What would it avail me if I had a brother who was a wise man, and I were a fool?

He continues:

> The Heavenly Father brings forth his only-begotten Son in Himself and in me.

In his study on Hindu Doctrines, **Rene Guenon** devotes a chapter to the relationship between theology and metaphysics. In particular, he writes:

> Every theological truth, by means of a transposition dissociating it from its specific form, may be conceived in terms of the metaphysical truth corresponding to it, of which it is but a kind of translation.

This needs to be kept in mind, especially for those who are put off by theological language or can only see arbitrariness in theological disputes. Thus it is instructive to try to understand the metaphysical meaning of this passage, especially considering that it is the fundamental premise of Christianity. "Word" is the translation of the Greek philosophical term Logos, of which there is no really suitable translation; hence, we shall leave it untranslated. There are two principles in play here.

- **God**: Principle of Being (Aquinas)
- **Logos**: Principle of order (Greek philosophy)

The identity of God and the Logos thus implies that the principle of order is inseparable from Being itself. Were that not so, then chaos would be on equal footing with order, not the absence of order; ignorance would be equivalent to gnosis, not its opposite; revolution would be a possible option to hierarchy, not a revolt against being itself; darkness would be in perpetual opposition to light, rather than its shadow.

Birth of the Logos in the Soul

> The Spirit blows wherever He wants, and you hear His voice, but you do not know where He is coming from nor where He is going; so it is with everyone born of the Spirit. ~ John 3:8

The breath of the Spirit is the pure act of intelligence, arising from the Silence. So how do you hear his voice? We read in *Meditations on the Tarot*:

> The pure act is unknowable in itself; it is only its reflection which makes it perceptible, comparable, and comprehensible; in other words, it is thanks to its reflection that we become conscious of it.

The Spirit is active principle and the Virgin is the passive, reflecting principle, like the calm surface of a body of water. It takes the two conditions for the conscious experience of the Holy Spirit, or Kingdom of God. As Jesus tells Nicodemus in his nocturnal visit:

> Amen, amen, I say to you that a man cannot enter the Kingdom of God without being born of Water and the Spirit. ~ John, 3:5

The Water represents consciousness. The reflection of the pure activity of the Holy Spirit will be distorted unless that consciousness is itself pure. Two qualities are necessary, one pertaining to the Mind, the other to the Will: it must be

- **Virginal:** free of false ideologies, beliefs, and dogmas
- **Immaculate:** free of the cloudiness of the imagination, passions, and personal desires

Reintegrated consciousness, the Kingdom of God, or the Primordial state requires a rebirth in the Spirit and Water, to be able to hear the Spirit and reflect it accurately. This is how the Word expresses the Silence.

The Word is made flesh by the Holy Spirit through the Virgin Mary.

Meditation on the Incarnation

At this time of year, it is certainly *de rigueur* to meditate on the meaning, actuality, or possibility of the Incarnation of the Logos in Jesus Christ. This will involve brief excursions into the implications for a spiritual path, metaphysics, and the radical change in the world process in the current cycle.

Of its actuality, I am sure all readers are familiar with the story; if not, it is easy enough to find. There will be objections to the story as miraculous and incredible, but these objections can only arise from an a priori commitment to a positivist world view that cannot prove itself to be true. If, on the other hand, one is ready to accept the actuality of unusual preternatural or supernatural phenomena, e.g., miraculous cures, amazing powers of yogis and tulkus, the skills of magicians, etc., then the story of the birth of Jesus cannot be so easily rejected. There is only the "vexed theological question of grace"; some will be willing to see it, others will not.

However, in this meditation, we are not as interested in the Incarnation as a matter of faith, but rather as gnosis. We will stipulate it as a given, and move on. As one of our mottos indicates, "truth lies in the interior of man" (St Augustine). Augustine moved beyond Neo-Platonism when he came to the realization that the Logos of the Greek philosophers, understood in an objective and exterior way, was actually the same Logos Who was incarnated and is known in man's interiority.

The Path of Affirmation

This is expressed in the Path of Affirmation that is conceivable in the Incarnation. All previous forms of spirituality follow the path of denial. Specifically, these would include Advaita Vedanta, Buddhism, and Neo-Platonism. This path ultimately tries to transcend the material conditions of life, including the human person, by the realization of one's true identity as Brahman or the One. In this path, any determination is a limitation.

In the Path of Affirmation, on the contrary, God is approached through these determinations. St Athanasius describes the Incarnation: Not by conversion of the Godhead into flesh, but by taking of the Manhood into God. This differs from the Oriental ideal of an Avatar in which a god takes on the appearance of a man for a specific purpose, e.g., Parashurama, an avatar of Vishnu, appeared in order to overthrow the rule of the Kshatriyas.

Instead, the Logos raised the human up to God, once and for all. Christ, as the second Adam, restored the possibility of the Primordial state—the Edenic state prior to the Fall—to man. On this Path, man is not annihilated, so that only God remains, but instead there are two who are united. Although largely ignored in common practice, this is an essential element of the catholic, apostolic, Roman religion. Some quick examples, although many more can be found, including the official Catechism:

Irenaeus: The Word of God, our Lord Jesus Christ, who did, through His transcendent love, become what we are, that He might bring us to be even what He is Himself.

Clement of Alexandria: The Word of God became man, that you may learn from man how man may become God.

Of course, the premier example of this teaching is Dante's *Divine Comedy*, where he shows us the path to union with God through the rich imagery of his poetry.

In Christian Hermetism, particularly as evidenced in our near contemporary, Valentin Tomberg, the birth of the Logos in consciousness is the result of the alchemical marriage between the Holy Spirit and the purified soul. That becomes the new, or absolute self, in union with the Father, or absolute being.

So, the goal of this path is the spiritual and alchemical transformation of man, and even the world. Ultimately, no one can be convinced of this through any type of rational argument, so this is only an invitation to follow that path. Once any type of realization of this nature is reached, one's faith is secure.

The World Process

In the literature on tradition, most of the attention is focused on metaphysical teachings that aim to transcend all material circumstances. There is lip service to social organization, viz., the idea of castes and hierarchy, as well as the notion of cycles of the four ages. However, the relation of metaphysics to the world process is often left unclear; to those who are striving to be liberated from all worlds, what difference would it make?

But, if the real path is the Path of Affirmation, then it does indeed make a difference. In the idea of the four ages, there is often the misconception that the ages run according to some independent and objective cosmic clock. If that is true, then one can be passive and simply wait for events to occur. In particular, the end of the Kali Yuga comes at the prescribed moment apart from any consciousness of it. That is indeed odd for a teaching that regards consciousness as primary over the physical and material. If that were true, then Guenon's call for the establishment of a new elite would make no sense.

All traditions recognize three forces: the three gunas in the Vedanta, or the Great Triad of Taoism. We will stick to the Western formulation of Providence, Will, and Destiny. Destiny is the automatic and deterministic element of the world process. Its law is that of increasing entropy; left to its own devices, the world winds down, ultimately to a totally undifferentiated state. This is compatible with profane science.

Of course, such a state is impossible, since nothing could occur in it and God is Infinite possibility. Providence is God's or Heaven's influence on the process, not through force, but rather through suggestion, persuasion, and creativity. This opens up new possibilities, especially the possibility for a new world to follow the old when all its possibilities have been exhausted. The middle term in this is the Will of man, responding to Providence and transforming his being and that of the world.

Creation and Redemption

The pagan view of cycles was defective. It regarded the world as uncreated with no beginning and man as perpetual. Hence, cycles reoccurred, in perpetual return, the same thing over and over. Even Guenon rejected this, since, in his view, a world had a beginning and an end, the end of one is the beginning of another, much different, world.

This we take as closer to the truth. Hence, we must understand the cycle, from a perfect age to an ever more degenerate one, and finally to the birth of a new age that is both in continuity with and different from its predecessor. This must be understood as a drama involving God, man, and the earth, not as the predetermined result of a mindless process, or even worse, some demiurge.

Hence, the transition from a golden age to a lesser one, did not happen according to some calendar, but was rather the result of man's will. On the other side, the transition from the kali yuga to a golden age cannot happen from within the world process but rather it must be interjected into it from a transcendent or providential source, to then be adopted by the Will of man, at least by some who will be the leaven.

So the Incarnation is the beginning of the process of Redemption, that is, the regeneration of man and the world in an age to come. That is why Valentin Tomberg could regard Creation and Redemption as the two great magical acts since magic "requires the perfect union in Love between two distinct and free wills: the divine and the human".

We know creation interiorly through the memory of the Primordial state and its loss. There is the testimony of saints and mystics, there is the evidence of it through perduring vestigial preternatural powers of the soul; ultimately, conviction comes through our own remembrance of that state.

Similarly, for the Incarnation. We know that there have been saints who have reached the divine union in this life, the Western equivalent of the *jivanmukta*. We, too, may have been graced with a taste of that union.

Have You Ever Drunk the Silence?

Concentration without effort ... is your life tossed to and fro by random events, thoughts, feelings? Or do you live life consciously? It begins with Silence ...

Rene Guenon claimed that at times when the authorities had lost the inner meaning of things, initiates would pose as jugglers or horse traders. That way, they could travel from village to village, under cover as it were, to meet with other initiates. One can imagine them carrying Tarot cards as a teaching tool, since they appear to be a harmless game, and are much more compact than transporting a library. That is how I see the first card: *Le Bateleur* (the Juggler or Magician) as an itinerant initiate. The name of the card is a French pun on "the low deceives you" ("*le bas te leurre*"), but the initiates are not deceived.

The Multiple States of the Being is Rene Guenon's fundamental work on metaphysics. In it he explains that "just as Unity (Being) is nothing but the metaphysical Zero (Non-Being) affirmed, the Word is Silence expressed." That is, Silence contains within itself the possibility of the Word.

But the Silence is more than the word. The latter is silence expressed, but Silence must needs include the inexpressible as well. Hence, Silence is related to mystery, which refers to something inexpressible, not incomprehensible (which is a common misconception). The implication here is that the understanding of a mystery requires intuition, a direct knowing of the inexpressible; what can be expressed can, on the other hand, be known through discursive thought.

Guenon makes an interesting etymological connection. The Greek *mysterion* derives from *myein* which means "to be silent". The same root *mu* in Latin is used in *mutus*, "mute", but more significantly in the word *mythos*, "myth". So a myth refers to that which is inexpressible, that is, something that can only be expressed indirectly by means of symbolic representations.

In *Meditations on the Tarot*, this Silence is related to concentration without effort. To know this Silence is *to be* this Silence. That is, the discursive mind is quieted of its thoughts, images, desires. This is a concentration, not *of* something, but the effortless concentration of the Silence. We read there:

Valentin Tomberg relates this card to "concentration without effort", reminiscent of Taoism, which is the necessary first step on the journey through the deck. Our Friend writes:

> Concentration *without effort*, which means there is nothing to suppress and where contemplation becomes as natural as breathing and the beating of the heart, is the state of consciousness — of the intellect, the imagination, the feelings, and the will — a state of perfect calm, accompanied by the complete relaxation of the nerves and muscles of the body. It is the deep silence of desires, concerns, imagination, memory, and discursive thought. We would say that the entire being has become like the surface of calm waters reflecting the immense presence of the starry sky and its inexpressible harmony. And the waters are deep, oh how deep! And the silence increases, always increasing, what SILENCE! Its growth takes place in regular waves which pass, one after the other, through your being: one wave of silence followed by another wave of deeper silence, then yet another wave of even deeper silence ... Have you ever *drunk the silence*. If so, you know what concentration without effort is.

Christmas and the Winter Solstice

> But unto you that fear my name, the Sun of justice shall arise, and health in his wings: and you shall go forth, and shall leap like calves of the herd. ~ Malachi 4:2

> The Sun of Righteousness, who drives His chariot over all, pervades equally all humanity, like His Father, who makes His sun to rise on all men, and distils on them the dew of the truth. He has changed sunset into sunrise, and through the cross brought death to life; and having wrenched man from destruction, He has raised him to the skies, transplanting mortality into immortality, and translating earth to heaven ... deifying man by heavenly teaching, putting His laws into our minds, and writing them on our hearts. ~ **Clement of Alexandria**

The West has always been a Solar civilization. Traditionally, it was the responsibility of the priestly caste to determine the calendar. In particular, Julius Caesar, in his role of High Priest, reformed the more ancient Roman calendar so that it would correspond more closely to the actual solar year. Nevertheless, a small error in the Julian calendar had led to a larger discrepancy in the course of centuries. Hence, the calendar was reformed again in 1582 by Pope Gregory XIII. In our secular age, the role has passed to the scientists who are adding leap seconds to the year whenever they deem it necessary.

Julius Caesar, in his calendar reform of 46 BC, did indeed set the date for the Winter Solstice on December 25. Over the centuries, the subtle error in the length of the Julian year gradually moved the astronomical date backwards. When Pope Gregory reformed the Julian calendar, he coordinated the Vernal Equinox with a later year, corresponding to the year 325 of the Council of Nicaea, rather than the original year of 46 BC. Thus, the Winter Solstice moved back to around December 21 instead of the original December 25.

In ancient Rome, the Winter Solstice represented the day of the new sun, inaugurating a new cycle. Like Virgil, who first led Dante on his journey, the rising of the Sun, the unconquered God, *Natalis solis invicti* finds its consummation and fulfilment in the Sun of Righteousness. The ancient Romans had anticipated the mystery of resurrection, the birth or rebirth of a beginning of "light" and new life. Only at Christmas, was that fulfilled.

> The true light that gives light to every man was coming into the world (John 1:9)

The mystic Johan Gichtel showed that the subtle Heart of man corresponded esoterically to the Sun. So, just as Jesus was born under the Sun in the macrocosm of space and time, he dwells in our heart.

Psychology of Mystical Experience

> We can indeed know that the bosom of the Father is our own basis and origin, and that our life and being find therein their life and principle. From this basis that is proper to us—that is, from the bosom of the Father, and from all that lives in him—shines forth an eternal brightness, the generation of the Son. And in this brightness, which is the Son, God sees himself openly, with all that lives in him. All those who, above their created being, are raised to a contemplative life, are one with this divine brightness. They are that brightness itself, and they see, feel and discover, under this divine light, that according to their ideal or uncreated being, they are themselves this abyss of simplicity, the brightness whereof shines without means in divine modes. Thus the contemplatives attain their eternal exemplar, after whose image they have been created, and they contemplate God in all things, without distinction, by a simple gaze, in the divine brightness. ~ **John of Ruysbroeck**

The concluding chapter of *Studies in the Psychology of the Mystics* by **Joseph Marechal**, S.J. deals with how one's world conception colours mystical experience. As a methodological principle, Fr. Marechal is not concerned with the truth of the metaphysical systems, but rather with its psychological effects. The obvious problem with his study is how to define "mystical experience", since Christian ecstasy and yogic Samadhi are often included as such experiences along with trances induced by hallucinogens, ritual dance, and so on. This, then, is his definition of **mystical experience**:

> Mystical experience is a religious experience which is esteemed as superior to the normal: more direct, more intimate, or more rare.

The corollary is that there are three fundamental elements:

1. A religious doctrine—rational or revealed—which is a metempirical doctrine, relative to the Absolute.
2. Psychological facts of actual experience that are relatively rare or exceptional, and susceptible of a religious interpretation.
3. A synthesis of doctrine and psychology which interprets the psychological facts as a function of the doctrine.

Not unlike Rene Guenon, Fr. Marechal accepts the ideal of a unique metaphysic, despite the historical existence of a variety of metaphysical systems. Given the three elements, the highest and purest expressions of mystical experience will be associated with an intellectual understanding of the ideal metaphysic. Fr. Marechal describes several metaphysical systems and the mystical experiences arising from them.

Animism

Inferior systems have not yet achieved a unity of thought from the plurality of sense impressions. An example is animism which postulates metempirical "souls" behind the world of outward experience. The medicine man or sorcerer will associate strange subjective states with these hidden entities. This includes experiences, among others, such as:

- Dreams with a sacred content
- Narcotic-induced delirium
- Trances resulting from extreme physical ascesis
- Hysterical ecstasies brought on by music or scents

Although such experiences are valued very highly and are still sought after by a substantial number of spiritual seekers, Fr. Marechal considers them not worthy of an extended treatment.

Metaphysical Awakening

Fr. Marechal points out the close connection of metaphysics with religion in general and with mysticism in particular. He uses the famous panel from the Sistine Chapel showing Adam's attraction to the finger of God pointing at him as the artistic rendition of the awakening of human intelligence to the notion of an Absolute distinct from himself. It shows:

- Man's consciousness of his own ego, at once infinite and limited
- His perception of the universe
- His thought seeking the Absolute

This is the Great Triad: the ego, the universe, and the Absolute. The relationships of these terms are the sources of two fundamental things:

1. The source of his potentialities of action in the physical order
2. The law governing his attitude and the key that unlocks his destiny in the moral order

Different metaphysical systems define those relationships in different ways. Although Fr. Marechal does not mention this, it is obvious that, as a practical matter, two sciences are a great help in developing those potentialities: esoteric cosmology, which deals with the universe, and esoteric psychology, which deals with man's inner states of consciousness.

Dualism and Pessimism

Dualist systems see the universe as the expression of the conflict of two eternal principles: e.g., Being or the Good vs non-being or Evil. Such viewpoints lead to destructive asceticism and negative mysticism. That is, one's destiny is determined more by the attempted renunciation of the "evil spirit" rather than by a path of positive and uplifting stages. The world is experienced a being limited by the unreal or not-being. The universe is seen as evil and illusory.

Marechal refers to Arthur Schopenhauer's philosophical system, although not strictly a dualism, but as a pessimism. The will to live creates a universe of "my" representations, which is nevertheless evil and meaningless. Only the renunciation of that will can be the solution. Again, beyond the negation of phenomena, there is nothing positive. In Manichaean, and even Buddhist mysticism, object, actions, etc., are all limitations; that is the sole Evil. Such mystical practices focus on overcoming the limitations of the World of Becoming, without consideration of what lies beyond in the World of Being.

Pantheistic Monism

This is a more advanced of sophisticated metaphysical system, what we may call the God of the philosophers. There is no opposition to Being; rather primacy belongs to the Absolute, which is beyond duality. The earliest such systems derive from the Upanishads or Vedanta. The essential basis of this philosophy is the identity of Brahman and the Atman, which is the sole reality. The apparent multiplicity of things and souls is illusory. Hence, man's destiny is to extirpate in his soul the illusory multiplicity of objects and acts to end up within the Atman. The Atman is known, but not as an object. Hence, the only goal is to "be" the Atman.

Comparable Western systems never quite go that far, since the idea of an ascent to God via created things is not denied. The influence of Plotinus affects not only the West, but Sufism and even Indian philosophers. God, or the One, eternally creates the world by casting out his rays like a sun to the "very confines of non-being". Then the things, which are divine fragments, have a desire to return to the unity of the absolute Good.

The human soul is between the pure Ideas and matter; it is attracted towards the Centre by Love. If love predominates in the soul, it begins to be concentrated. Firstly, it apprehends intelligible beauty through the senses. Then by contemplation, it is purified and unified: "to contemplate is to become what is contemplated." From sensible beauty, the soul passes to the lower intellect of concepts, or psyche. Then it becomes the higher Intelligence, or nous.

Still the drive of Eros leads it to seek the perfect unity of the absolute Good. Thus it contemplated Being as the summit of the intelligible world. Yet, there is still the duality of Essence and Existence. Ultimately, through Love, even that duality is overcome in the One.

Later metaphysicians such as Giordano Bruno, Benedict Spinoza, or Johann Fichte are in this stream. For example, in the negative direction, Spinoza defines man's moral end as the freedom gained over inadequate ideas and the passions. Yet, there is the positive direction of the "intellectual love of God".

Fichte discovers the pure I, or spirit, opposing to itself the not-I, or universe, so that it may progressively know itself and conquer itself by gaining self-mastery. The human intelligence is raised to the dignity of an Absolute, i.e., a "mysticism of becoming God."

The point is that "metaphysics can invest the ordinary operations of our understanding with a mystical significance." However, Marechal identifies the mysticism that such systems inspire as purely "natural", achieved through thought, and lacking any notion of "grace". In short, the distinction between nature and supernature is obscured.

Monotheism and Supernatural Mysticism

Finally, Marechal address strict monotheism as the answer to the question of the relationships between the Ego, the universe, and the Absolute. God, then, is strictly transcendent without any common measure with that which is not himself. He possesses the fullness of Being which excludes not-Being.

The universe then is a "becoming" proceeding from God and arranged between the limits of pure Being and pure Non-Being. Although external to God, it is moved and directed by divine action. Finite things do not create themselves as in monistic systems; yet they are not evil or nothingness as in the pessimist dualist systems. They are free creations of love and possess value measured by their degree of participation in the perfection of the divine Being.

Hence, the created intelligences and wills tend to reproduce the divine Ideal and try to make progress towards it. Hence, mysticism from this view will have many analogies with Neoplatonism. Creation is grafted onto the closed cycle of the operations of Divine creation as an epicycle. At the beginning of the epicycle, the divine actions descend into the innermost elements of things, giving them their "nature".

Next the thing ascends back to God, as every material being "tends to the perfection of its species". The entire physical world tends toward vital unity in stages:

- The vital unity, through its comprehensive interiority, foretells and prepares for consciousness.
- Sensibility (or sense experience) reflects the unconscious world of matter and brings it to the threshold of the idea.
- Then, the intelligence recognizes the intelligible in the data of sense.
- Finally, it discovers in its "becoming" no other end except God himself. This closes the epicycle.

The return of things to their first principle, i.e., the ascent of the intelligence to God, is a mystical phase. All becoming has a *law*, and in that law, is an *end*. Marechal then describes that law as it is fostered in the depth of the human soul. There are two aspects: the order of intelligence and the order of the will.

The Intellect tends toward the assimilation of Being as know, or, Absolute Truth. The Will tends to the possession of Being as absolute Good. The two tendencies converge on the direct vision of God. However, insofar as the soul is restricted to the plane of creation, there must also be an initiative from God that expands the intelligence and reveals himself.

This initiative from above leads to states higher than what can be achieved through the natural mysticism of monism, as it opens up the horizons of grace and supernature. It does not reject the natural metaphysical systems, but builds on them. Paradoxically, it leads to unity with the divine while retaining the individuality of the soul. That is the highest achievement of the Western Tradition.

Summary

Marechal summarizes the three principal types of mystical theories:

1. **Negative mysticism**. A mysticism of simple liberation, the result of dualistic cosmologies and philosophic pessimism.
2. **Positive mysticism**. A mysticism of divine becoming immanent in the soul.
3. **Theistic mysticism**. The mysticism of objective striving toward God by means of knowledge and love.

Clearly, a superior metaphysic will lead to deeper mystical experiences.

www.ingramcontent.com/pod-product-compliance
Lightning Source LLC
Chambersburg PA
CBHW070802050426
42452CB00012B/2453